THE PORTAGE POETRY SERIES

SERIES TITLES

The Blue Divide
Linda Nemec Foster

Lake, River, Mountain
Mark B. Hamilton

Talking Diamonds
Linda Nemec Foster

Poetic People Power
Tara Bracco (ed.)

The Green Vault Heist
David Salner

There is a Corner of Someplace Else
Camden Michael Jones

Everything Waits
Jonathan Graham

We Are Reckless
Christy Prahl

Always a Body
Molly Fuller

Bowed As If Laden With Snow
Megan Wildhood

Silent Letter
Gail Hanlon

New Wilderness
Jenifer DeBellis

Fulgurite
Catherine Kyle

The Body Is Burden and Delight
Sharon White

Bone Country
Linda Nemec Foster

Not Just the Fire
R.B. Simon

Monarch
Heather Bourbeau

The Walk to Cefalù
Lynne Viti

The Found Object Imagines a Life: New and Selected Poems
Mary Catherine Harper

Naming the Ghost
Emily Hockaday

Mourning
Dokubo Melford Goodhead

Messengers of the Gods: New and Selected Poems
Kathryn Gahl

After the 8-Ball
Colleen Alles

Careful Cartography
Devon Bohm

Broken On the Wheel
Barbara Costas-Biggs

Sparks and Disperses
Cathleen Cohen

Holding My Selves Together: New and Selected Poems
Margaret Rozga

Lost and Found Departments
Heather Dubrow

Marginal Notes
Alfonso Brezmes

The Almost-Children
Cassondra Windwalker

Meditations of a Beast
Kristine Ong Muslim

PRAISE FOR

Restoring Prairie

"This a weighty, but often witty, collection of new poems by Margaret Rozga in which she invites us to walk the restored Waterville prairie with her through the great cycle of seasons and it becomes, for the reader, an unimaginable enjoyment. There are poems of the natural world and its green grace, but there are also poems of loss, of the death of family and friends that take their place alongside the history of prairie loss and restoration. She says, 'When grief re-awakens / you feed it.' The prairie becomes a sanctuary, a safe place that seems both outside time but also of it. And as we heal the prairie, we are also healing our hearts. Her poems give memory to all the particulars: the bee, the seed, the grasses and golden honey. And through them we are there, too."

—CARY WATERMAN
author of *Threshold: New and Collected Poems*

"'How to restore what was lost?' asks Margaret Rozga in the foreword to *Restoring Prairie*. From the 'sparrow song' and 'dry pond,' to the bedside of dying loved ones, to those hidden in the margins of history, these poems journey through grief toward places of hope. Speaking to who and what has passed, the poet writes, 'Maybe you inspired these words: rain, prairie, trill, ground, cosmos, wings....' But renewal is possible, she tells us, though it may take '... a long time.' It is, ultimately, 'A season of shedding. Of healing. To get there. To get here.'"

—LOIS ROMA-DEELEY
author of *Like Water in the Palm of My Hand*

"Believe in what you see and what you don't see, Margaret Rozga tells us in 'Lingering.' In this beautiful new collection, our attention is turned to the visible and the unseen. These poems honor what is present as well as what is not. *Restoring Prairie* also restores our hearts and faith through the poet's wisdom and compassion."

—JEROD SANTEK
Founding and Artistic Director, Write On, Door County

"Margaret Rozga's poems in *Restoring Prairie* reflect a tender, urgent yearning for restoration—personal, communal, and ecological. Reeling from the losses of the COVID-19 pandemic and of beloveds through the years, Rozga takes solace in a carefully restored scrap of 'city home prairie' that soothes her heart and reminds her to pause for nature's teachings. Confronting the indigenous displacements and environmental devastation that made Wisconsin, and in conversation with poets across centuries, Rozga's poems hauntingly sing of cumulative loss and the power of nature to bring truth to our wounds. 'How to restore what was lost?' the poet asks, and the answer arrives in a lesson the size of a bumbling prairie bee: 'Start small, but start.'"

—JENNIFER MORALES
author of *Meet Me Halfway: Milwaukee Stories*

"Restoration of lands back to pre-settlement terrain is growing in popularity and importance and as a practitioner of this work, I am reassured and stimulated by the work of Margaret Rozga. *Restoring Prairie* provides an introduction and then depth about how an area that was prairie for ages before European colonization, then farmed for generations, and finally set aside to be restored to prairie in the best way known. The poems skillfully interweave the plant, soil, and animal life with human. In telling the story of the plants and animals nearby, Margaret avoids speaking for them and has them express their own voice and reality. In the midst she steps out to tell more about life and death events in her own life and that of other humans. The trip from human stories to prairie is refreshing and set in words and emotions that make you feel and believe."

—MICHAEL MCDERMOTT
Co-founder and director, Black Earth Institute
Managing Editor, *About Place Journal*

"*Restoring Prairie*, a beautifully unified collection of new poems by Margaret Rozga, addresses ecological and cultural history based on personal engagement with farmland being restored with prairie species. The poet's emotional, philosophical and spiritual engagement with the place lend tremendous depth. Contemplating the pendulum of destruction and renewal, she juxtaposes poems of hope with laments for the extent of centuries of development, leaving a mere shadow of historic natural bounty. Other forms of grief are intertwined including the loss of loved ones as well as relentless warfare and the ongoing pandemic. Each adds moral complexity while heightening the impact of the collection. This book can be read as a hymn and prayer for healing, an act of conscience and a journey of the heart, calling above all for the courage to hope."

—CHRISTIAN KNOELLER
author of *Completing the Circle*

"The poems in *Restoring Prairie* by Margaret Rozga meditate on nature and death, move through time and generations of people. They instruct us how to be human and deeply alive in nature and in the moment. I am moved by the poems in this collection: the faith it takes to restore land to prairie, to live with so much heartache and loss, personally and globally. There are lessons on how to live, observe, be with the trees, plants, and other being with wings in creativity and hope. Lines dazzle, like 'The way forward here is poetry.' There is music and wisdom here, 'the cadenced chittering of chickadees,' and '... She may be this land itself speaking,' these are poems you will come back to, to be refreshed and remember what it is to be a poet and alive."

—ANGIE TRUDELL VASQUEZ
Madison Poet Laureate 2020-2024
Macondo Fellow

Restoring Prairie

Margaret Rozga

CORNERSTONE PRESS

UNIVERSITY OF WISCONSIN-STEVENS POINT

Cornerstone Press, Stevens Point, Wisconsin 54481
Copyright © 2024 Margaret Rozga
www.uwsp.edu/cornerstone

Printed in the United States of America by
Point Print and Design Studio, Stevens Point, Wisconsin

Library of Congress Control Number: 2024935796
ISBN: 978-1-960329-47-9

Cornerstone Press titles are produced in courses and internships offered by the
Department of English at the University of Wisconsin–Stevens Point.

DIRECTOR & PUBLISHER
Dr. Ross K. Tangedal

EXECUTIVE EDITORS
Jeff Snowbarger, Freesia McKee

EDITORIAL DIRECTOR
Ellie Atkinson

SENIOR EDITORS
Brett Hill, Grace Dahl

PRESS STAFF
Forrest Campbell, Carolyn Czerwinski, Sophie McPherson, Kylie Newton, Eva
Nielsen, Natalie Reiter, Ava Willett, Cam Williams

for Marlin Johnson

in memory of Gertrude Sherman

for all whose names have been erased from prairie history

ALSO BY MARGARET ROZGA:

Holding My Selves Together: New and Selected Poems
Pestiferous Questions: A Life in Poems
Justice Freedom Herbs
Though I Haven't Been to Baghdad
200 Nights and One Day

CONTENTS

3.

4.

5.

FOREWORD

The search for a beginning is a beginning.

Defeated in the 1832 Black Hawk War, the Sauk, Meskwakis (Fox), and Kickapoo were removed from the land called *Ouisconsin* by French traders. Of course, there is history before this. It may survive in traditional stories and in artifacts left behind, sometimes found by the newcomers, usually called settlers.

Among the newcomers were the young Swedish scientist Thure Kumlien and Margaretta Christina Wallberg who married when they arrived in Milwaukee in 1843. Accompanied by her sister Sophia, they settled near Blackhawk Island. Like their neighbors, they plowed prairie to farm. Unlike their neighbors, they did not disturb indigenous burial mounds.

Thirty miles to the east and six years earlier, George Hosmer claimed 346 acres of prairie near the crossroads community of Waterville. In 1843 he sold part of that land to James Meigs, who in 1844 built a house about a quarter mile from his Waterville Road frontage. In 1867 a third owner, James Thomas, took possession of what had become a farm. But I get ahead of myself. Not to leapfrog the story, in 1848 Wisconsin officially became a state.

In Germany that same year, middle- and working classes rebelled against the aristocracy. And lost. Some revolutionary Germans found their way to Wisconsin. One of them, Margarethe Schurz, in 1856 started the first U.S. kindergarten in Watertown, about twenty miles northwest of Waterville, and twenty miles due north of Blackhawk Island." Mayors in this worker-oriented German tradition led Milwaukee until 1960. What happened to that liberal tradition? A more vexing question: what happened to the indigenous?

Removal. Some people survived. Some managed to return, though their land was not returned. Much was lost. Culture. Prairie. Many old scars remain. Some newer are inflicted.

How to restore what was lost?

Restoring what was lost may start small, but start all the same. On the unfarmed old railroad bed, look carefully. Find enduring prairie grass and wildflower seeds. Gather them. Plant them. Each fall more seeds. The prairie the settlers broke begins slowly to take root again.

Along Waterville Rustic Road, today on the edge of going suburban, ninety-eight acres of former farmland are being restored to woodland and prairie. This is where I spent a year writing. Time spent, yes, but not lost. Time more than repaid. Here with other writers or alone is where again and again I come to be restored.

The way forward from here is poetry.

—Margaret Rozga
Milwaukee, Wisconsin
February 2024

1.

Márgarét, áre you gríeving
Over Goldengrove unleaving?

—Gerard Manley Hopkins, "Spring and Fall"

Waterville Prairie

Here near the banks of the creek, a white moth
flutters above a tangle of low-hanging green
branches. A tree inclines toward the grace
of the cold flow from the source spring.

Here in staccato flight a bumblebee, above
abundant goldenrod, purple asters and spent
milkweed, lingers at a low stem of clover.

Here in the thick green, *jrchp*, an unseen
single-note bird gives bounce to a branch in
the thicket. Near woods and restored prairie

here if you listen, if you stand still enough,
here if you quiet your desire for revelation,
here the shade of oak and pine will touch you
here often, maybe always, with green grace.

I am here

unmasked and outdoors
seeing two trees grown close
bridging the gap between them.

Having been isolated for more than two years
until our gathering in this open space
between the house standing here since 1844
and the new barn, built forty years later,
stone foundation, weathervane rooster on roof,

looking out beyond myself
to the stretch of restored prairie
to the woods, I fill a notebook with lines
of words that skitter toward meaning,

fill a sketchbook with timid drawings
that warm me to art, to art-making,
ways to bring to my city home prairie,
woods, singular and double trees.

Here
where the ephemeral pond is now dry, but
the creek, though low, still flows cold and clean,
I am.

You Are Not Here

May slipped away, its cool, its gentle buds.
June blossoms full heat and humidity.
I keep my voice low and calm as if
the person I speak about were with me,
as if we could still follow this boardwalk
edging Lake Henrietta together. And if we
heard a toad punctuate our talk, like the one
I hear now, we'd pause, forget our easy
summer planning to concentrate: where?

There, there in the weeds. See?

I am, of course, now the person speaking,
walking alone along the marshy uncertain
shoreline. I am, as well, the person spoken to.
The water calm, touch, touch, and turn.

Summer

Minus a friend to talk to
Minus a sense of purpose
With butterflies winging
on spiky purple flowers

Minus my own wingedness
With a map of who I was
With overlay of who I am
With a sense that if only

Minus a sense that all
is right with the world
With a dream, with
a full and aching heart

today on the trail

the sun blinds me   I turn

walk into my shadow

What Is Present with Me

I'm standing next to our bed in our house on 41st Street, saying farewell
to my dying husband. I am eating a bowl of oatmeal with apple
slices, raisins, and chopped walnuts. I am sitting next to my dad in a
waiting room at St. Luke's Hospital, waiting for word of my mother's
surgery. She did not make it.

I am standing next to my dad's bed in that same hospital.
I say, *I'm sorry for all the trouble I caused you.*
He says *you kids were never any trouble.*
How can he not remember? My oatmeal grows cold. The doctors put my
father on a ventilator to keep him alive until my brother who is running
a marathon can get here.

I am with my dad who goes to see his mother who is dying. He goes to her
bedside; I wait in the kitchen, impatient. Uncle Syl tells me to be quiet,
to be more like my sisters, to behave, to understand what is going on. I sit
down at the table, but there is nothing to eat. I am eight years old. I am
21. I am 40.

I grieve, but I do not understand. It is one thing to stand
vigil with someone dying. It is another to pass into being
the one remembered. I finish my bowl of oatmeal, feel full.

Equinox Blues

Nothing
stays in balance
one equal day and night
in spring tips to day
in fall to night
oh, yeah

English Sparrow

"The first known introduction of the species to Wisconsin occurred in 1869."
        —R. Tod Highsmith

I want the wellness of then, the health
of then, its ripeness, my careless
assumption of forever of then.

Lots of then stashed in my closet: bank
statements of then and even then-ner than
then; bills, receipts, cards, tributes and
awards from then, of then; slim and thick,
shy and bold, ephemeral then-ness.

A trio of sparrows flutter upward.
Descend. Up. Again back to earth.

Death is so then. Why did I not see that before?
Even as I saw death: mother, husband, dad,
friend. Then it was them. Then I had no
reason to anticipate my own then. Even
then. Even now, I'm able to hush then
into a thin maybe then.

Then comes knocking on my door, but I let then
think I'm not home. Let then hang his/her/their flyer
pamphlet, brochure, calling card on my doorknob.

Then is no longer the live-happily-ever-after *then*.
My friend, my would-be friend, the one I did not
hug at the gathering because I didn't want to let
the baba ghanoush on the pita bread I held in my hand
smash onto his shirt, he, too, is wrapped up in a *then*.

Then we are each alone with invasive sparrow
flutter, ubiquitous, ripe, sparrow song.

Power

close to Marlin's house
energy unseen   musters

amasses   rallies
strikes

thundering spring
storm
splits
red   cedar

drills down
to phone line
cuts it

dumbfounds us

Slant of Silence

When grief re-awakens,
you feed it, cradle it
in your arms,

carry it up
the uneven path
above the creek.

Grief is these deep,
dense woods. Trees
fork, branch, block sun.

Words are tinder.
If grief were to speak,
how much would it burn?

During the Pandemic

She tweeted a plea for cute
puppy and kitty photos.
Chubby babies with happy
faces, tiny hands reaching
for tiny feet: these would help,
she said, ease her soul struggling
with quick-to-trigger events
on each evening's news.

Not to mention stories of refugees
fleeing a foreign power seeking
to expand across borders even if
it means reducing cities to rubble,
leaving debris to be cleaned up
who knows when, who knows by whom.

She struggled to keep the evil from seeping
into her soul. She refrained from exploding
at irritations: delayed payments of small sums
she's owed; people coughing, sneezing,
breathing on her as the virus peaks again;
events planned as maybe; neighbors
crabby even when they try not to be;
offending parties voted back into power.

Confined mostly to home, mostly alone for well
over a year, she felt her heart, her mind shrivel
to virtual reality. Where to refresh, restore, renew
inspiration? She needs living, breathing presence.
Dare she hope?

She tells herself trees were greening again,
the prairie would soon bloom orange, purple,

gold. She turns off the TV. She eats healthy
food. She pleads for cute kitty tweets as if
tiny and furry were at least refuge if not remedy,
as if beauty were stronger than guns, stronger

than disease, as if we could return to health
like it seemed the rest of nature had done, was
doing. She'd seen it at the Field Station,
the prairie. Of course, she tells herself,
the prairie.

Mulberries

She sees the barn, the mulberry tree, the cat;
walks down to the creek, writes what she sees,
writes, she says, in grief, says so far much of what
she has written this morning is, her word, *drivel*.

Drivel. The word jumps hopscotch in my head, keeps
my pen poised near my still blank page. I believe
among her words, maybe among mine, the possibility
of play. *Drive* already in the soil of her word.

A word, even an unpromising one, may be
a seed. Some of us see the barn, the mulberry
tree, the cat, and don't see them. They stand,
they shed berries, they rub against your legs.
No wonder in that. And yet,

though word-deprived, beyond the present grief
I believe underfoot like fallen mulberries, drive
words take root here near the barn, there near
the wood-fired kiln built into the hill, or
in the woods, ripe, and waiting to be pulled up
from the damp soil along Scuppernong Creek.

Brief Grace

She walks the path
toward the ephemeral pond.
At least she believes the path she took,
the one on her left, is the one she wants.
She hopes to hear the deep longing calls
of frogs. Last night's thunderous rain
surely replenished the waters, renewed
those throaty and resonant songs.

Why I'm Here

I say I came to see the trees grow, but
in the grasses across the creek, what moves?
Squirrel? Yes. Fidgets. Scampers up.
Disappears. Reappears. Jumps thin branch to

thin branch as if
they could hold
its weight. Look—
look! They do.

In the berry-laden branches of bushes nodding
in the wind toward the creek, an orange bird.
Oriole? Appears. Disappears.
Another brief, surprising grace.

A Prompt

I draw the farmhouse in faint pencil lines
as if I'm afraid of my own talent,
as if it will disappear before

I find words to grace,
to complement,
this page.

In the eaves, a wasp's nest.
A wasp emerging, wings
almost invisible, legs
thin as pencil lines.

What I don't see—
its ability to sting—
packs power.

Draw bolder, I tell
myself. Write fast, enjamb
emphatic lines, leave
an itch.

Rain

Clinging to fine tooth-edged leaves,
rain drops sparkle in the slant of sun.

Another band of this storm forecast,
but dark clouds move south, southeast.
Sun slants from the west. Believe
what you see.

Bird song. Believe
what you hear. Know
that even a language
you don't speak pleases
between rain and persistence
of late afternoon sun.

Even dare believe you have power
to weather a passing summer storm.

Just think—
I almost stayed home.

Her Gesture

By the time a phrase musters into a sentence,
it may be false. By the time my journal entry rises
above the page, a plane taking off, almost
as soon a plane aborting take-off.

I owe it to myself to pay attention, to be
glad at the arrival of small birds' flutter
and song. Up a branch, down a branch, fly
to the next tree, repeat. The sun angles higher,
or the earth tilts to allow a higher angle of sun. Yet

men want to shatter
other men and,
in the process,
endanger the earth. Yet,

bird song. The angle of sun. Yet
a couple walks the path beyond the creek,
crosses Waterville Rustic Road, heads
toward Henrietta Lake, she with a paper cup
in both hands, held to her chest like a chalice.

2.

The UWM at Waukesha Field Station:
a place where plants and animals can live
to reach their natural destiny; where oaks
and pines can live for 300 years or more;
where dead trees can rot in peace;
where death contributes to new life.

—Marlin Johnson, first Field Staton director

Her Story

Gertrude Sherman did not want a gravel pit
across from her home on Waterville Rustic Road.

How to stop expansion of the neighboring
gravel company to these ninety-eight acres
too hilly, too small, too unprofitable

to continue as a farm? An idea dawned—
Ms. Sherman, ever a teacher, decided
to purchase the land she did not need
for herself and donate it to the university.

The reward for her generosity? A neighbor
equally committed to education and the land,
newly hired biology professor: Marlin Johnson.
He saw, before its new life, what this land could
be, a place for learning woodland and prairie.

He collected seed, organized friends, directed
construction of low-key classrooms, a building
bearing her name, tells students and visitors,
tells us, her story, her unfinished story. We
may be writing the middle. Whatever leaf
we write, we also write to restore, to renew,

to keep these woods, pond, creek, purple aster
and goldenrod, these prairie stories growing.

Write-Ins at the University Field Station

Some of us sit at picnic tables,
some of us bring our own chairs.
Most of us look for a spot in the shade.
Then some draw, most of us write

maybe about the Field Station,
its cup and compass plants,
the 200-year-old oak,
the ephemeral pond,
Lake Henrietta (Marlin says
it's a glacial excavation
without an inlet or outlet—
really a pond, not a lake)
now choked with growth
such facts, seeds for our art

maybe about what's beyond this prairie:
rumbles of civil discord,
assault rifles,
war, wars,
grief, grieving (Sara says
her mother; Suzanne says
her mentor; I say husband,
dad, mother, friend, friends)
drought, wildfires
indictments, convictions
such sorrows, the soil.

We write, we draw. Here
not to escape, we bring all
with us, sometimes find
in due time, inspiration
blossoms like wildflowers.

Orchestral

because orchestras
aren't always there when we need them
—Bob Hicok

An oriole perches here on the prairie,
a guest soloist who leaves soon
after the concert, flies north
where others will incline their ears
to hear this melodic delight.

I would not deny them this pleasure.

For cardinals and for raucous cranes,
please applaud, and chickadees
whose soothing song like rhythmic verse
all summer long stays with us.

Spring

In Lake Henrietta's shallows
two toads. One jumps
onto the back of the other.
Their bodies are perfect—

the pattern of their skin
taut over flesh, over bone,
slim and powerful legs
not presently in action.

At the sound or the vibration
of our footsteps on the boardwalk
first one,
then the other, jumps
into the tangle of green
that obscures the shoreline.

We turn, head back toward the prairie,
crossing the road, following the path
into the abundance of maple trees
wildly flinging wingéd seeds.

Feast

Reach for mulberries
growing along the trail
Recall your childhood
mulberry song   Now see
not bush but tree   Delight
in rhyme   Eat   Appreciate

Oak Opening

A lone oak stands despite the odds it faced against the plow
that broke prairie to farm, a seedling unseen or strong enough
to resist uprooting. Amidst acres of corn, it managed to grow,
a mistake somehow uncorrected. Some mistakes, we later see,
were always a blessing. This resilient one grew tall, taller, grew
to be valued, spreading its branches, reaching wide, shading the
farm then and now this restored, this restoring prairie.

large lobed bur oak leaves
glorious green grace   branched wide

words catch in my throat

Another Prompt

A yellow jacket climbs
the page opposite the words
I slowly pull out of the air.

It pauses mid-page.
I stop writing.

When it flies into the wind
I inscribe it on this page.

Winds

This morning's rain as gentle as breathing,
this morning's coffee stronger than usual.

Yesterday afternoon's writing, scarce words.
Last week's escalation of guns, of war, of wars.
The year's rain multiple inches below average.
This decade's shrinking horizons,
this century's dire predictions.

This day's seeds, roots, sprouts,
growth. This life's forward-looking,
and its hesitation to look forward.

This pause to focus
on a gold finch on a power wire.
This moment's stillness, a slight
tickle of wind, these yesterdays
tucked away. The future still malleable.

This morning's breathing now
gentle as soft and welcome rain.

No need to hurry

I tell myself as the world spins
and others stir up a flurry,
people raging with inner volcanoes.

Ask a tree about slow, about growth,
the cadenced chittering of chickadees,
the flight of larger ones. Sit here

in the presence of warm air and
breathing greenery. Feel how deeply
everything breathing wants to live.

An unseen owl in the distance.
Another human walking the prairie
stops to talk. She, too, brings with her

a history, her own, and that we share.
We are separate branches of a tree.
This morning air holds nighttime cool.

Start small. Tiny seeds gathered in October
planted in April, may grow, then, come summer,
bring the bee nuzzling—see there!—in the center
of the well-rooted cup flower, restoring the prairie.

I don't know your name

You crawl along the edge
of my canvas bag. Another
like you skitters around
my box of pencils. You

with your translucent
wings fix yourself
in one position and are not
dislodged when I shake
the handle on which you rest.

I brush you away with the tip
of my pen. You do not take flight.

Do you know you have wings?

Late June and Love in the Air

Above quick flowing
Scuppernong Creek
dragonflies
slow
dance in
mid-
air

Hope is a stalk of purple asters

at the edge of the tall grass. Hope is a plot
of flattened grass where perhaps a deer
lay last night. Hope is a puddle at the side
of the trail filled with this morning's rain,

the twiddle of a leaf on the quaking aspen,
the reach of the oak shading the trail
up the gentle slope to the prairie,
the dense ridges in the bark of the tree.

Jeff says *before dark more bird song.*

Hope is the bird song that begins with a crow
three-point, four-point call, call, call, call,
answer call. Hope is a human
melodic whistle, a small white dog
the human catches up in his arm,

the blue stem seedheads, their rise
from green-gold to tawny-almost-red stem
their slight bend from the wind, from
their own weight, the graying of the clouds.

Hope is a tri-branching goldenrod arcing
over the purple asters, a bee nuzzling blossom
to blossom. Hope is another and another,
a butterfly mostly black, red sumac close
to the ground, soft pine needle branch
jutting out from near the bottom of the trunk.

Hope is a slope, a swale, a swamp, a sibilant insect,
a sweep of acorns on the path beneath the reach
of the oak, and on the path that angles
toward the deep pine woods, what I think a rabbit hole.

Barb says *I sketched again at the top of the hill*
and I'm sorry if you missed it—a crane—

just as she names it, again the fricative dissonance,
like a tractor grinding gears, deep belly breath grating
scraping, scrapping, bellowing through long narrow neck,
un-song, un-music, unmistakably crane.

It did not sound another note. Still, it spelled hope.

Maybe You Are

"Maybe after the funeral
you became a butterfly on a baby's head."

—Nikki Wallschlaeger

Maybe after the funeral you spread your wings. Maybe you are
the split of a seed on the tomato sprout. Maybe you are
the pink and purple cosmos that, released from a crowded pot
and transplanted into the garden, spread to fill the empty ground.
Maybe you are the trill of a redwing blackbird. Maybe you are
not outside at all, but the spider on the hallway wall. Maybe you are
a word at the end of a line in a prize-winning poem. Maybe you
inspired these words: rain, prairie, trill, ground, cosmos, wings.
They line up here in reverse order. Re-ordering is a key to living.
Yesterday and the day before I walked the prairie not in the afternoon
fallow hour, but in the early morning. Maybe you are the early sunshine.
Maybe afternoon rain. Maybe I need not be angry with you any longer.
Maybe that anger is sweet.

I am

on the path to the creek
Surprise!
grasshopper leaps
reaches my knees
again and
again

Mid-Summer

This week purple coneflowers
are in abundance where
they were not so last week.
What do I know of abundance?
Knowing is always smaller
than the abundance to be known.

Thure Kumlien knew the way
of naming created by Carl Linnaeus,
brought it and his keen mind
from Sweden to this land
now named Wisconsin.

Names offer one way to know
what you see, what you hear.
Other ways bloom
in wildflower abundance.
Score the chorus of bird song.

Note the cadence of chickadees
in the soft abundance of their music
to your ears, and when it ceases,
hear, know profound, abundant
silence.

May His Memory Be a Blessing

Robert Parris Moses
(1935-2021)

A flurry of small birds
at the height of the tallest pine:
te tseh tse tseh, like the swish
of brush on surface of drum.

I do not know who drums,
who sings, *tweh, tweh,*
tweh tweh. I hardly hear myself
and that may be a good thing.

Yesterday, July 25, 2021, Bob Moses died.
Bob Moses, born in Harlem, educated at Harvard,
civil rights worker in Mississippi, beaten
by opponents of voting rights who failed

to deter him. He turned 1964 into Freedom Summer.

History, hard and soft as it is, details get
smudged, erased, its lessons unlearned, untaught.
He turned algebra into a civil rights project,
won a much-deserved MacArthur genius award.

Each russet tassel on the prairie grass
nods, keeping time in the soft breeze.
I'm not describing the intricacy of tall
blue stem well, and that is only a start.

Now he walks this prairie,
he haunts the halls of Harvard,
he practices philosophy in New York,
he takes refuge from the draft in Tanzania,

he's in Mississippi, Freedom Summer's 50th
anniversary, talking with Milwaukee teens
who, since first hearing of his work, hoped
to meet Bob Moses. The distance deciduous.

Hawk aloft in the updrafts, wings extended.
When the prompt is to write about yourself
as rock or bird, most choose bird. *Freedom
of course*, they say, the ability to rise,

to rise above what holds them back.
Overhead a crane. Its song raucous
in a way I won't try to render. In Mississippi
I met Bob Moses before I met him.

He led. I joined the march.
We have been there, and now
we're here and we're every place
we've tried to see beauty, tried to sing.

Imprint of Bark

I press palm against rugged,
deeply grooved bark. Marlin says,
This tree is over 200 years old.
It saw passenger pigeons.

I look at the impression of the bark
on my hand, see palpable power.
Roots anchor, extend, reach deep
into the earth, source of power.

I suggest we write letters to the tree.
Suzanne asks, *What would this oak*
want to hear from me?

This question grows in me
and over the summer, answers—
that I love its shade.
that I admire its bark,
and the graceful curve
of its lobed leaves,
that I'm awed, humbled
by its longevity, that I'm gratefully
alive with the oxygen it provides.

In the fall the ground is graced with acorns.
By year's end I am always talking to this tree,
even when I appear to be talking about
this tree, even when I'm not at the Field Station.

Its roots and my roots, yours, too
touch, intertwine, somewhere
unmapped, under where we stand.

I carry the image, the imprint of its bark
as if it were a line of poetry, as if
it were a poem I committed to heart.

Drawing at the University Field Station

Barb draws blue lines in the trunks of her trees.
She says *it's watercolor. Painting.*

Beyond the art, beyond the scarce words
and thick woods of this sacred place,
I fear another war looms.

The trunk of one tree arches over the trail
that leads to the ephemeral pond. It is not
now the season for water. Sooner or later.

The leaves of the aspen quake in the wind,
a back-and-forth motion like a hand
signaling indecision.

Later I walk the path along the creek, see
the tree she painted with watercolor pencil.
The blue, she says, for contrast, for depth,

a sense of the tree's intricacy even at surface.
I've known such intricate, such saintly blue.
If we can avert the war, I may know it again.

Weather and Climate

We are in a war of words, reinforced by bullets. We are
in a shooting war, reinforced by words. We answer
questions not knowing what we're asked. We write
answers without knowing the questions. We repeat
ourselves. We almost repeat ourselves. We are
in the first of winter. We are in the season
of fall rains. Trees bare their tangle
of branches. Rain freezes. Rain
softens, whitens. Still the war.

I should be able to write a protest poem

I should be able to write a poem
about Afghani interpreters deserving better,
being dangled the delicate hope of asylum
for whatever that is worth.

I should be able to write
with the insistent beat of a heart on fire,
the passion of Whitman's barbaric yawp,
the precision of an accountant
totaling the debt to be repaid.

Airlift Afghan allies to the Field Station
where I write of black-eyed Susans
counting their thirteen brilliant petals
flower after flower, utterly dependable.

We should. I should. What is power for?
What are words for
if they do not set deeds in motion,
if they do not celebrate good,
if they do not open up space.

If they allow moral failure
if they do not uncover names
of the unnamed who erect
obstacles to justice, then

I cannot write a protest poem.

Rhyme is

how I twiddle my thumbs
how I pace the floor when awake
at four o'clock in the morning

Do bees sleep?
Do deer appear like miracles?
Do giraffes laugh?

how I fall asleep instead of counting sheep

Can opossums smell blossoms?
Does a tree see me?
Do flies vie for prizes?
When is an ox quicker than a fox?

how I dream *everyone knows an ant can't*
becomes *an ant* can *move a rubber tree plant*

how I wake aware there's internal rhyme
in Afghanistan

I can't reach across half a globe
can't cancel the chaos of a collapsed regime
or insure flight of families out of strife
into a new life

Rhyme is the flawed way I now pray

What depends on a blue

wheelbarrow?

Marlin loads it
with logs

cut from invasive
buckthorn

& stacked at the shed.
Quick

back to the house.
Warmth.

Sun, Table, Chair

—*after Lois Roma-Deeley*

You've grown smaller after all these years.
You're Kafka taking another step away
from the castle. That is what grief will do

to you. In the heart-breaking clarity
of August sun, your words also fade
and shrivel, a hollyhock gone dormant
after this year's deepening bloom.

A bee lands on the picnic table. You take time
to look. Transparent wings folded against the body,
the bee walks the length of these painted planks,
not taking, not now, the possibility of flight.

You admire the intricacy of its two forward eyes.
That it has three more eyes you take on faith,
uncertain how and where to look for them,
uncertain also of your two-eyed power
to see. Nevertheless, you lean forward.

3.

This is to remember
the names
we've given away
or never received.

—Denise Sweet, "Constellations"

revery alone will do

—*Emily Dickinson in "To make a prairie"*

Dear E.,

When prairie shrinks to revery
it leaves a bitter taste, sorry
to say, bitter as yesterday's coffee
reheated.

When you fold prairie dreams
into the singularity
of one blossom and one bee,
then contract them even
further, no matter how sweet

the notion, you've reduced
your vision, words, and maybe
even (I hope not) your soul. Revery
is dream-drift backwards, memory
romanticized impressionistically.

So much better imagination that leans
toward the future, what we could be.
Your disappearing prairie at least
may hold a seed to be replanted

and connected with what buzzes, breathes,
colors, surprises, excites, and reassures,
which is to say more than either
of us, certainly more than me.

I stir honey into my cup of tea,
and for the honey, I depend
on clover and on bees.

Remembering Beauty

1.

When Emily, age thirteen, a student at Amherst Academy
and not yet a poet, Margaret Fuller, twenty years her senior,
also Massachusetts born, was more daring and keener to explore
the Wisconsin Territory still intact with bees and clover,
visiting all the beauties of the adjacent lakes—Nomabbin, Silver,
and Pine, neighboring Waterville. She proceeds, as does
the Scuppernong, to *the Bark river, which flowed*
in rapid amber brightness...

2.

Juliette Magill Kinzie, also keen and daring and newly married,
traveled the Fox River to Fort Winnebago, on the strategic
point of portage to the Wisconsin River before the 1832
Black Hawk war: *a more exhilarating mode*
of travel can hardly be imagined than a voyage over
these waters, amid all the wild magnificence of nature...

3.

Black Hawk remembers: *We always had plenty—*
our children never cried with hunger, nor our people
were never in want. Here our village had stood for more
than a hundred years, during all which time we were
the undisputed possessors of the valley of the Mississippi,
from the Ouisconsin to the Portage des Sioux...

Restoring Words at the Wisconsin Center

Go the way of earth
and women
into lyric matters

—Carl Rakosi

Give me your indecision
where you can't pray or sing
Flee like arrows that expanse of
you must do, over and over

Don't argue, just exchange
sorrow, rage, bricks, joy, old brooms, cats all
larger-than-life-size
Go the way of the earth

We all travel the Milky Way together
Look at the stars
Light curls itself, its brightness inward
It has a silver face
its music gentle wisdom
and tinkle of singing ice
the last word of every sentence

Let it hover there like the dare of a cat
All big, pulsing, turbulent, panoramic
always hoping
it is the life in our hearts

Respect yourself, honey

So endlessly, and tenderly, you do it
day after day
Dreamer, I think
if you are not afraid
a hawk flies up, settles on a fence post

dream-tracks cover the land
this bridge into the future
If I cd just get a word in edgewise
there is a history to the land
to trembles / in the tendrils

My eye is on the water
the Wisconsin waterways
around which direction never changes
surely waterbirds will alight
here for the first time
amid all the wild magnificence

Can you / will you say, do you know / are you
homeward bound at last

I sit on the steps of our small house
All I know today is that I am
in my grandmother's kitchen
fully free
to wait, to learn
to dance, to go to work
to love the forgotten

૪૯

*Acknowledging the authors included in this cento in the order of
their appearance:*

1. Peggy Hong
2. Bruce Taylor
3. Michael Mooney
4. R.M. Ryan
5. Karl Young
6. Margery Latimer
7. Horace Gregory
8. Carol Rakosi
9. John Muir

4.

Woman be a powerhouse
A light bulb during a blizzard storm
A canvas full of ocean and song
A portrait in the sun

—Destinny Fletcher, "From a Door Worth Opening"

She says

she's a painter. She says she's a poet. She says
she's a social justice advocate. She might not say
that she is not what she used to be. She might admit
privately that she is not a dreamy-eyed girl, not

anymore, not a believer in what anyone tells her,
not susceptible to flattery. No indeed. She says
mindfulness is overrated. She is mindful. She is
awake to suffering, awake to beauty, hopeful

in her sad way, which is to say she carries
a lot of history, its weight almost unbearable,
which is to say she is alive. She is not here to say.
She is at the restored prairie seeking what colors,

lines, brush strokes. What touch, what texture.
What awe in this afternoon's certain slant of sun.

Restoring the Prairie

Hope is goldenrod in an arc
over a stem of purple asters,
a bee nuzzling blossom to blossom,
a proliferation of tiny white petals
centered in gold, one solid orange line
across the wings of a black butterfly.

We walk unpaved trails crisscrossing
these acres of restored prairie. Hope
is your naming the beauty I paused
to admire though I didn't know
its name. Between our knowing
and all our unknowing, hope grows.

Knowing

I am the green in the seed unfolding
breaking through composted soil
reaching for the sun
becoming

Hawk and Haiku

The next poem is almost always far away.
The next poem may appear at any moment.
It may be in the heavy segment of torso
of the insect that fixes itself
on the handle of your canvas bag,

or with the black ant
following the grain
on a wooden plank
of this picnic table.

Or maybe in the yellow blossoms
amidst the tall grass, or the hawk
gliding in updrafts of warm air
between pine and maple.

Absent a hawk, imagine
the scallop of its extended wings,
the tapered shape between them.
This one won't fly away. It will fly.

* * *

you are far-sighted
extend your wings   ride the wind
swoop down   you've got it

No one wants to leave

We shed the layers
we wore for warmth

In our sketchbooks
we draw, erase, draw

layer color, shape
slant lines, rhymes

Sun arcs south to west
We gather in a circle, share

our shadows
our blind spots
the words they drive us to

Sara's pencil points upward
as she awaits her next word

She says pine needles are shed
in late summer to early fall, before
the deciduous drop their leaves

I linger, write into the dark
the last to close my notebook

Lingering

In a near dark sky over leaf-strewn ground,
the waning moon powers through cloud,
merest arc of moon, but enough
to infer the whole. Meditate on the moon.
Meditate on earth looking up at the moon.
The moon in my photo looks smaller
than it does, than it did, to my naked eye.
Believe in what you see and what you don't see.

See the space between them. See the earth
covered in snow the color of the moon.
Clouds shape-shift in currents of wind.
I walk the edge of the creek, my way
softened by fallen pine needles,
brightened by this slight margin of moon.

Congregation

I didn't get that, she said.
No, it was this way, he said.
Maybe not, the third said. And
a fourth: *How about lunch?*

Their voices, among others, scamper
through my mind like a congregation
of squirrels chasing each other up trees,
flinging themselves from branch
to roof and for a while out of sight.

This may be what is meant by eternity,
the silent resonance of words long after
we think them stilled. I think them stilled.
I can't be certain of the plural we.

Nevertheless, I am more
than me, more than singular,
what with all these voices within me,
maybe mine out there as well.

Plural

My shadow and that of the tree to my right
and slightly behind me are cast forward
shading the path to the barn. I have not
seen myself in quite this way before—
I should have known—I am not alone.

A Gain

I am everyone I dream—
the girl threatened,
the vulnerable one,
the one growing thin
as paper,
and the girl defending her,
coaching her, coaxing her,
writing her brave.

where on the prairie

do you see commas
semicolons   hash tags
asterisks parentheses
quotation marks dashes
let alone periods   What
does this say about
the need for punctuation
marks when

hold on

all you really need is space

cardinal

slip beneath declarative
interrogative   imperative

how to get there

shortshortshort long
long long shortshortshort
long shortshort

exclamatory   I wish
I spoke bird   It takes
time   silence   a good ear

In bloom

after the space
of four fallow years
oh praise
the hollyhocks

joy of jaunty pink
deepens to red edges atop
rambunctious
green stems
the way words
in due time
sometimes flower

a double triangle

flutter of orange above

late august asters

In September

as I walk downhill
to Scuppernong Creek
a single syllable
jrchp
then a bounce of a branch
in the path-side thicket
A lone bird in the bush
quiets my desire
to have one in hand

Tenacity

above a circle of prairie
flowers bowing downward
a white moth flutters

perches briefly
on underside of flower

flies off   returns
holds on

Scuppernong This Fall

The name like a bird song
short short   long   a cardinal's call
maybe one unseen in a nearby tree

When the rain came this week
five inches   swift   the algae bloom
at the bend in the creek that worried me
dislodges   the water regains its momentum
streams free again cold and clear

Marlin says the aging septic systems
of houses upstream, built around the lake
created by damming the creek, likely
emit their contents into the ground,
then leak into the creek.
Scuppernong pays the price.

Scuppernong   like the rhythm
of its name   the cadence
of a cardinal's territorial call
flows free and clear   for now

October on the Prairie

Purple asters still hold their color
A west wind urges   frees   shakes loose
sweeps gold maple leaves from branches
rains them down to earth
after taking them
for a spin

You ask   *do you still believe*
the arc of the moral universe
bends toward justice

The moral universe   I want to ask
is it contained within   or bigger
than the unmodified universe

What of the 130 years
this prairie was broken and farmed
What of the 50 years now of restoring prairie

I seem to have brushed up against wild parsnip
A blister above my right ankle
Some salve   a dressing — I believe
in healing and keep going—

Yes   I still believe
the arc of the moral universe
bends earthward with the pull of my hands
and   if you will   the pull of yours

Look up

See between
clouds
it's blue
like a lake
flowing into a river
and opening
again a lake

Who Is *She*?

Of course, my colleagues: Barbara,
Meg, Suzanne, Teresa. And those who
inspire, Denise, Juliet, and Margaret. *She*
is the women present with pen, with paper,
with love and keen eye: Sara, Karen, Maria,
Carol, Karen, Marie, Kay, Eloisa, Adrian,
She is the prairie they pay attention to. *She*

is the surprise of a pasqueflower in early spring, a steady
compass plant in July. *She* is one of the pair of cranes
who walk in front of me on the classroom path. *She* may be
the bee that walks the picnic table behind Marlin's house.

She is the glacial excavation lake we call Henrietta
because we do not know her ancient name or if
she enjoyed centuries of anonymity.
She is the ephemeral pond.

She may be the women unnamed in history who worked
the farm and kept house a quarter mile from the road.
She could be the indigenous women erased from
this land. *She* may be this land itself speaking
all the women who have loved her.
With my longing to hear,
she may be me.

5.

I am a world within a world manifesting spring.

—Megan Muthupandiyan

Update

Thure Kumlien brought with him
from Sweden to the Wisconsin prairie
from his professor, the great Carl Linnaeus,
a system of naming and a desire to name
the new in terms of that system.

Meg demonstrates a plant identifying
app on her cell phone. Thus we learn
plant names, one way to begin seeing.
These, her phone also tells us, are also
often called Michaelmas daisies.

That name claims an old-fashioned English
overlay for a proliferation of tiny open-faced
blooms spraying forth from each single stem
in a myriad array. But these fall asters

are native. Bees seem to ignore us
our history, our name seeking.
They hum, touch, linger, rub, snuggle,
jive, nuzzle, nestle, pollinate, create.

Marlin's Garden

Today is the soil, yesterday
the compost, tomorrow
the abundant splitting of seeds
with energy to push through
the hard (or rain-softened)
earth.

The hopeful among us celebrate
the sprout, the leafing, the bloom,
welcome bees, butterflies, this earth-
centered miracle, this composted
present.

Seed Gathering

Today the gathering of prairie seeds,
walking through bluestem grass, we
pause beneath a beloved oak's reach,

close friends, distant neighbors, colleagues,
Marlin's students who, when possible, return
to this community restoring prairie.

Wind, rabbits, dogs, deer, chance mostly
might free seed to find new ground. We
assume a purposeful place among these.

Engaging in this common work, I leave
at least briefly my singular pen, release
my solitary page, my singular I, rise. We
face each other, the seed gathering us.

After and Before Writing

Stop!
say the prairie grasses
in their October gold.

Look up
from the desiccated curl
of grounded oak leaves,
says the jewel blue
span of sky slanted
with late afternoon sun.

I set down my pen.
Breathe.

This moment
holy
both before
and after words.

Melody, Harmony, Song

Tcheh tcheh   a gentle call
short vowels   soft consonants
amid wind-whispered leaves

Then one *swp*   quiet   more *swp swp*
My transcription not quite right
what letters what alphabet

Slight sway of tasseled grasses
in soft breeze sings color sings
silence   A monarch   a moment
on the hem of my jeans

Walking the Prairie

You do not have to say anything.
Your body is a word. Black-eyed Susans
speak in their color, their black, their gold,
their straight stems, their height, their abundance.

Even the solitary flower calls to be
observed. You think it calls to you,
but that says more about you
than about the flower you behold.
It speaks itself glorious. Bees listen.

Grasses bend their heads answering
the wind. This harmony. A cacophonous edge.
This symphony. A cardinal asserts himself:
yet yet yet again, so so so pay heed.

I am here at the prairie again
listening. My body, my ear.
Maybe for the first time, I hear.

A Moment of Awe

Every natural fact is a symbol
of some spiritual fact.

—Ralph Waldo Emerson

Let the prairie speak even if you hear imperfectly,
even if you want to impose meaning.

If Emerson suggests a one-to-one relation
between the natural and the spiritual,
I neither hear nor see that. Yet he may be
onto something in his authoritatively
imperfect way.
     I come not to simplify.
not to take anything, not to receive, but to ease.
I come to behold.
      It takes a long time. A season
of shedding. Of healing. To get there. To get here.

Writing at Scuppernong Creek

I sat on a rock and stilled myself.
I watched an oriole alight on a branch,
turn, and fly away. I did not.

Growing wings takes time,

time I do not have. And I prefer, need,
am grateful for the weight, bend,
reach, handiness of my arms.

Song of Myself

I said I came to see the trees grow, which is to say
I didn't know where peace, how peace, what peace,
what blending of imagination and green and
flower and bluestem. Now that I've learned

a handful of names and beheld how color rises
and works and gives way, now that I've seen
the ephemeral pond flood and dry, now that
I've witnessed bumblebees nuzzle the centers

of asters, now that I've chilled when a poem
branches into prose and warmed when prose
turns lyrical, now as these lines break and build,
now as these fragments seek a main clause. Now.

Imagine now green where, now flower how,
now bluestem and now myself what. Now song.

along Scuppernong's banks

the fallen limb of one tree

rests in the arms of another

Of Course

Above and beyond
the 1840s house whose roof
and chimneys I see
on the rise of a knoll
branches sway, leaves
flutter in the wind.
In the sun, the undersides
of leaves look like white lilacs.

Of course, the greens meet, overlap,
the quaking aspen lighter than the oak.
Of course, the house is shorter than the trees.
Of course, branches, of course, leaves,
of course, steady, of course, wind and
nearly invisible trunks, and, of course,
roots which I cannot see at all.
Of course, deep roots.

On the way home

driving east on the freeway, an unpredicted rain. On the downward slope of the road nearing the city, the downpour too quick to clear and of course more than concrete can absorb, as if concrete could absorb anything, even noise. Traffic slows. At the edge of the rain, the edge of the city, the edge of the clouds, the sky to my right opens sun-filled blue. And more. Wide, close, fresh, vivid. A rainbow. Just to the north, to my left, it doubles. Calm, intense, calm, so near each other. My gratitude for this, for their unpredicted grace.

at the county line
thundering change of weather
then rainbow doubled

Forward

In this city cold, I savor what lingers
in mind of green and tawny warmth,
milkweed, compass flower, aster, each
in turn in bloom. Relief from the heat
beneath the oak's reach. At Scuppernong Creek
an oriole, and, especially, flying across the prairie

a solitary crane, calling perhaps to another.

I hold on to enough in this chaotic time
to take me into, to take me uneasily,
to take me with a lot of baggage,
to take me prairie-calmed, yet
city-centered to seek, dare I say to help
plant, peace from prairie seeds.

Seeds

This Sunday's brief sun.
Warmth. Redwing blackbird
trills. Tiny seeds. Planting dreams.
Growing hope with, in, on,
for the earth

Leaning on luck

weather and promises
despite mid-week chill.
Teetering on hope,
the way I imagine
peace will sprout.

Field Station April

I am here. Again
field station spring.
Oaks on the open prairie
not yet oak round, oak full.

Potters gather to fire their work,
stoke the capacious kiln built
into the hill behind, below, the barn.
Shapes of clay—

vases, Barb's with a triangular mouth,
two others bottomed like garlic bulbs,
sets of plates, bowls, pitchers, some
with broad, some with narrow spouts—

intense and prolonged wood heat
hardens them, projects ash that
finds, clings, marries the clay,
beauty other and more than

anticipated. Chanced beauty.
I look upward, swallows circle
the barn. I look outward. Oak,
leaf in promise.

Before We Leave, A Word / Or Two

A touch of gold, but the oak still holds / its green
as if this is the margin / of summer.
Quaking aspen / already bare-branched.

My heart keeps pounding / its rhythm.
I almost have something to say / a word
on the tip of my tongue, no, not / even there,
in the back of my throat, in my   /   churning belly.
For now, these   /   marginal words.

On these margins, I walk ahead   /   a child
stepping gently at the edge of the lake   /   the irregular
border where waves break / on shore
before retreating and becoming / once again
indistinguishable lake.

Celebrate water.
Celebrate water's reach / and retreat.
Celebrate sand.
Celebrate soil in all its textures / loam, clay,
mud, silt, all   /   the earth.

Some people write / themselves large,
some small.
The prairie is both those people.

All the earth / the way
it sends up trees / and calls
their leaves back onto itself / the way
it makes words / catch / in /   our throats.

You are a song

The morning opens.
On Sawyer Road a crane,
slim and stately as Abraham Lincoln,
but it takes more than a minute
for the crane-ness to register.

Its buff-blond color at first
seems only a glint of sunlight.
Then it moves. It has legs. It has eyes.
It turns its head, faces me.

I forget my worry about the truck
slowing behind me. Surely the driver
sees, stopped here on this narrow road,

the crane, silent energy,
and me, energy humming.

We are a song.

ACKNOWLEDGMENTS

I am grateful to the journals that first published the following poems, sometimes in slightly different versions, sometimes with different titles.

"At the University Field Station." *About Place Journal*

"Before We Leave, A Word / Or Two," Wisconsin Fellowship of Poets Calendar, 2024

"Hope is a stalk of purple aster at the edge," *Presence: A Journal of Catholic Poetry.* A video version of this poem was included in the Woodland Pattern Book Center's online Poetry Marathon, January 2022, recorded there and posted on YouTube.

"I am here" (previously "I Am"), *Portage Magazine*

"I should be able to write a protest poem," *New Verse News*

"In September," *tiny wren lit*

"Lingering" (previously "Clouds are ephemeral, not so the moon"), *Creative Wisconsin Magazine*

"Look Up," *tiny wren lit*

"May His Memory Be a Blessing," *Pensive: A Global Journal of Spirituality & the Arts.*

"Maybe you are," *Leaping Clear*

"Mulberries," *Bramble*

"No need to hurry," *Where The Meadows Reside*

"October on the Prairie," *Flyover Country*

"Restoring the Prairie" (previously "At the Field Station"), *About Place Journal*

"Rhyme is," *Oxeye*

"Seedlings," *Whale Road Review*

"Walking the Prairie," included on a poster in shop window for the Poetry Walk, Sheboygan, Wisconsin, April 2024.

"What depends on a blue" (previously "Warmth"), *tiny wren lit*

For their continuing work to restore prairie and woodland, many thanks to Teresa Schueller and William Schneider.

Thanks also to Emerson Lehmann, reporter for CBS58 Sunday Morning, whose thoughtful questions led to insights that became the themes shaping this book. "We don't want it to be a secret anymore": UWM at Waukesha Field Station is a hidden treasure (cbs58.com).

My deep appreciation to Eloisa Gomez, Karen Haley, Suzanne Joneson, Barbara Reinhart, Sara Sarna, Karen Schleicher, Maria Tammi, Danielle Wucker and all the artists and writers who joined the Write-Ins at the Field Station, finding and sharing inspiration there.

Heartfelt thanks to Dr. Ross Tangedal for his inspiring work as director of the Cornerstone Press. Many thanks to Madison poet and artist Wendy Vardaman for the cover image and to Forrest Campbell for the graceful cover design that suggests the movement in the wind of tall prairie grasses. Profound gratitude to the editorial team for the attentive care they gave these poems. Ongoing conversations with senior editor Grace Dahl were valuable and fun. She and editor Kylie Newton, editorial director Ellie Atkinson, and proofreader Cam Williams asked insightful questions and offered suggestions that without a doubt made this a far better book than it would otherwise be.

MARGARET ROZGA is a life-long Wisconsin resident and the Wisconsin Poet Laureate from 2019–2020. She is the author of five full-length poetry collections, including *Holding My Selves Together: New and Selected Poems* (Cornerstone Press 2021), which received an honorable mention for the Edna Meundt Poetry Book Award at the 2021 Wisconsin Writers Awards. Her work was nominated for inclusion in the 2005 *Best New Poets* anthology and for a Pushcart Prize, and her first book, *200 Nights and One Day* (2009), was awarded a bronze medal in poetry in the 2009 Independent Publishers Book Awards and named an outstanding achievement in poetry for 2009 by the Wisconsin Library Association.

Rozga has also been a resident at Shake Rag Alley; the Sundress Academy of the Arts; Write On, Door County; the Sitka Center for Art and Ecology; and the Ragdale Foundation, as well as a creative writing fellow at the American Antiquarian Society. She lives in Milwaukee.

www.ingramcontent.com/pod-product-compliance
Lightning Source LLC
Chambersburg PA
CBHW022102020426
42335CB00012B/791